Heidrun Liepe

The Neues Palais

Frederick the Great's Guest Palace in Sanssouci Park

with contributions by
Stefan Heinz,
Rosemarie Hofmann
and
Barbara Spindler

Prestel
Munich · Berlin · London · New York

CONTENTS

The Neues Palais – The Last Great Palace in Sanssouci Park

Frederick II (Frederick the Great), by Franke, c. 1765. From war to art: immediately after the devastating Seven Years' War, Frederick—portrayed here in his general's uniform with his face etched by strain—embarked on his most extensive building project, the Neues Palais. In Franke's painting, armour and laurel wreath are lying behind him and the dagger is mere ornament. Frederick is pointing towards the Temple of Janus in the background: in ancient Rome the gateway of the temple was closed in times of peace.

With the start of work on his new summer palace, Sanssouci, in 1745, Frederick the Great (1712–1786) made the town of Potsdam his primary royal residence. His great-grandfather, the Great Elector, had chosen Potsdam as a second residence alongside Berlin and set in train a busy period of building in and around the town. In his childhood Frederick had got to know the austere beauty and openness of the landscape on the River Havel. The view of the Havel lakes from the "desolate hill" had made a lasting impression on him. Frederick's years in Rheinsberg in the Mark of Brandenburg were probably his most carefree. Here, as crown prince, he was at last able to pursue his interests: his days were occupied with philosophy, music, theatre, literature and architecture. He was surrounded by gifted artists in an atmosphere of mutual inspiration. In this period he planned his own royal residence in Berlin, the Forum Fridericianum on Unter den Linden, with his architect Georg Wenzeslaus von Knobelsdorff. Just as the temples and triumphal arches of the Forum Romanum had once symbolized the dominion and power of Rome's imperial rulers, the architecture of Frederick's Berlin was to serve as a manifestation of sovereignty. With his decision in favour of Potsdam, however, Frederick abandoned his original plans and brought only the Berlin Opera House to completion.

In 1744 Frederick—now king—ordered vineyard terraces to be built outside the walls of Potsdam and that winter chose the City Palace in the centre of Potsdam as his winter residence. The following year the foundation stone was laid for Sanssouci, which came into use as a summer palace in 1747. Official receptions continued to take place in Frederick's other palaces in Potsdam, Berlin and Charlottenburg. For family celebrations, the court gathered at Charlottenburg.

Following a lengthy interruption, Knobelsdorff once again accompanied the king to Potsdam in the early 1750s. Plans for a large palace were revived. A site south of Sanssouci on a bend of the Havel perfectly matched the architectural criteria of the Baroque. The park was extended to the west, where the central avenue was to end at a grotto. By the start of the Seven Years' War in 1756 planning was already at an advanced stage under the direction of the king. However, in 1763 Frederick the Great decided on a different site: the Neues Palais ("new palace") was to form the western end of Sanssouci park. The long years of war had weakened the king's health. This may have been the reason for abandoning the original site by the river, or the decision may have been due to the difficulties that arose with the purchase of the site on the bend of the Havel.

As Knobelsdorff had died in 1753, Frederick the Great commissioned Johann Gottfried Büring to plan the Neues Palais. The magnificent complex that resulted continues to astonish those who see it even today. Büring, who had already worked under Knobelsdorff in Potsdam, took over the direction of the royal department of works in 1754 and from 1763 the construction of the

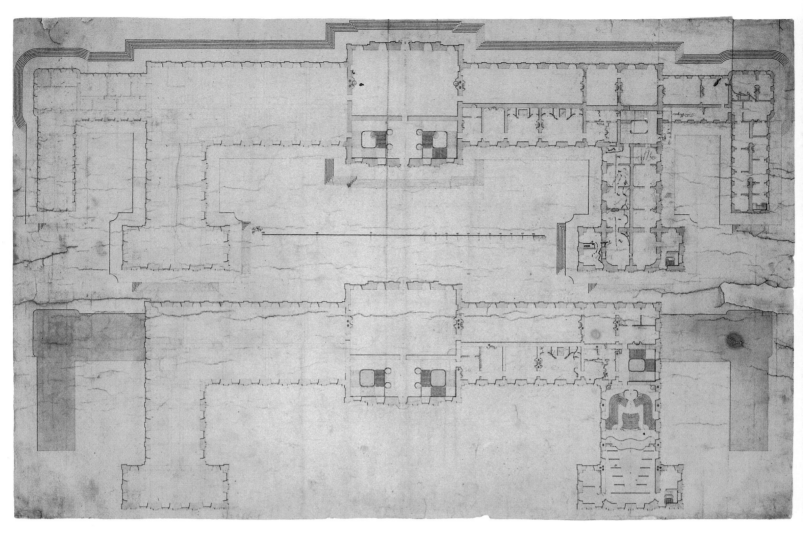

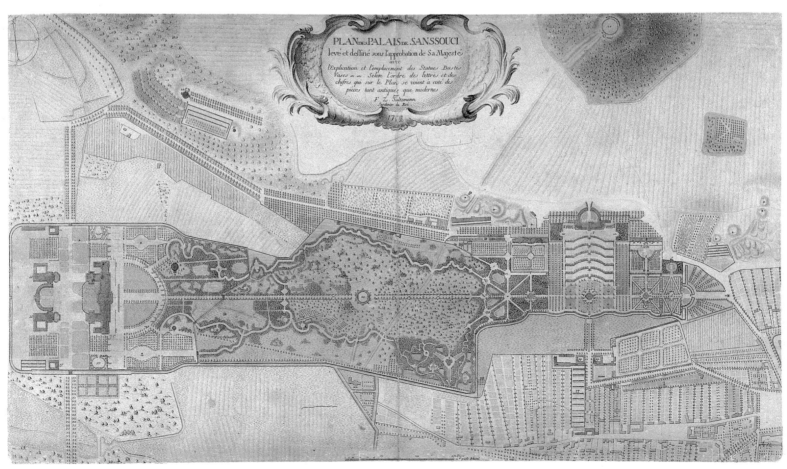

Above left: the architect Carl von Gontard (1731–1791) designed the ground floor and first floor of the Neues Palais in 1765/66. The annotations are by the architect and the king himself.

Below left: the court gardener Friedrich Zacharias Saltzmann first surveyed Sanssouci park and later drew a plan, which appeared with explanatory notes in 1772. A semicircle 150 m in diameter, which was adorned in summer with about 80 orange and bay trees, adjoined the garden façade of the palace. The canal, originally constructed to transport building materials, also served to drain the marshy ground. To the south of the palace was a riding circuit, to the north an open-air theatre. The Temple of Antiquities and its counterpart, the Temple of Friendship, concealed behind trees, form the transition to the garden.

Above: the view of the palace and deer park from the ridge to the north shows the imposing complex after its completion. On the avenue of mulberry trees in the foreground Frederick the Great rides a white horse behind a procession of carriages. This view was painted in 1775 by K. C. W. Baron, who also worked on the interior decoration of the Neues Palais as a painter and gilder.

Following double page: the garden façade of the Neues Palais. In accordance with Baroque tradition, the parterre garden is next to the building. The bay trees reinforce the effect of the wide central axis.

Neues Palais. However, he fell out of favour in 1764 and was replaced by Carl von Gontard, who a year previously had come from Bayreuth with other artists and entered the royal service. At the time of his arrival work on the palace was in full swing, the Corps de Logis having reached the height of the first storey and work also having begun on the south wing, housing the royal apartments. Jean Laurent Legeay had meanwhile also produced his designs for the Communs, a pair of magnificent domed buildings intended to accommodate the kitchens, utility rooms, members of the royal household and servants. At the same time the Communs formed an imposing backdrop which obscured the view of the wilderness behind. Gontard, taking Legeay's design as his basis, connected the two buildings with an impressive colonnade culminating in the centre in a triumphal arch. The resulting space, true to the tenets of Baroque architecture, embraces the courtyard of honour and the so-called Mopke, a square paved with bricks laid on their sides. With this imposing palace complex, Frederick the Great demonstrated the power and strength he had newly acquired in the Seven Years' War to a Europe which only a short time before had expected to see Prussia destroyed. He himself later once described the project as a "fanfaronnade", a blowing of his own trumpet. A large dome surmounted by the Three Graces, visible from a great distance, crowns the main wing of the palace. In 1754 the king spent time incognito in Holland and, according to Manger's *Baugeschichte von Potsdam*, was deeply impressed with the Dutch manner of building. Originally the whole façade of the palace was to have consisted of red bricks with white mortar. As it proved difficult to procure the materials even for the south wing, the king decided that the main wing should be plastered and then painted brick red. The "mortar"

between the "bricks" was painted in white. Pilasters of sandstone stretch over two and a half storeys to structure the façade in alternation with the reddish brick pattern. The surrounds of the doors and windows are richly decorated in relief. Sandstone sculptures, representing scenes and figures from classical legend, stand in front of the pilasters and on the parapet and balustrades. More than 400 statues and putti were executed by a host of sculptors, including the Räntz brothers from Bayreuth, Johann Gottlieb Heymüller and Johann Peter Benkert, who also worked on the Gemäldegalerie (Art Gallery) and the Chinese Pavilion in Sanssouci park.

Previous double page: the Upper Vestibule forms the official entrance to the staterooms and the Upper Princes' Quarters. The light red marbled walls and the stucco-marble columns lend the room a quiet elegance. The ceiling painting by Johann Christoph Frisch (1738–1815) portrays Venus the goddess of love and the Graces, surrounded by winged cupids.

Left: Frederick the Great dispensed with a single
grand staircase in favour of four smaller flights of
stairs, thus permitting his guests separate access
to their private apartments.
Above: at the express wish of the king, the façades
were embellished with rich sculptural decoration.
Some 400 sandstone figures adorn the palace, carved
by a large number of artists, including the Räntz
brothers from Bayreuth.

The two single-storey wings were also topped with domes, each
decorated with a gilded Prussian eagle. In order to be able to use barges to
transport the vast quantities of building materials, such as the large blocks of
sandstone from Pirna in Saxony, a canal was built to link the construction
site with the River Havel. This canal was later included in the landscaping of
the palace grounds. The construction site itself was marshy, and elaborate
foundations had to be laid to bear the weight of the palace complex. The king's

ideas did not always accord with those of his architects. Their collaboration was often marked by tensions. For example, the king thought the foundations much too high. Earth was piled up to bring the appearance of the exterior into line with his wishes. The interior floor plan of the Neues Palais was entirely dictated by its function as a palace for guests. Carl von Gontard was principally responsible for the interior design of the rooms and halls of state. Entry to the palace was by means of four grand staircases, which permitted separate access to the guest apartments. The architectural highlights are the galleries and halls of state in the central section of the palace. The palace theatre is situated in the south wing. The mezzanine floor was allocated to the gentlemen and ladies-in-waiting. For himself, the king had summer apartments installed in the small south wing. After a remarkably short construction period of no more than 7 years, the 300-room palace was completed in 1769. The Neues Palais was the last major building project to be commissioned by Frederick the Great.

The main entrance to the Neues Palais with its court-yard of honour surrounded by railings and the Mopke, a square paved with bricks placed on their sides.

The Temple of Friendship (built 1768–1770) is situated in the grounds of the Neues Palais. Frederick the Great dedicated this spot to his favourite sister, Wilhelmine. Famous pairs of friends from classical antiquity are portrayed in relief on the columns of the temple and make allegorical reference to the friendship between the royal brother and sister. Margravine Wilhelmine of Bayreuth was one of the cleverest women of her time.

The Palace and its Residents

Frederick the Great (1712–1786)

The writing closet in the royal apartments.

The marble bust of Frederick the Great in the bedroom of the royal apartments. It was sculpted in 1770 by an unknown artist and shows a man aged by the hardships of war.

The composition of the Baroque palace complex suggests that the royal apartments are situated in the central tract. However, the king did nothing to fit in with these expectations. For his private apartments he selected the small wing at the south end of the building, far away from the official areas of the palace. It is typical of Frederick the Great to have gone against the usual ideas about demonstrating his status. His sparkling intellect, his enthusiasm for architecture and interior design are reflected above all in his private apartments. Along with the halls of state they are undoubtedly among the artistically finest of all late Friderician Rococo rooms. The king dispensed altogether with that major element of Baroque planning, the enfilade (the aligning of internal doors in a sequence). The state of his health had deteriorated greatly, and he hoped to reduce draughts by not placing the doors connecting his apartments along a single axis. This lends the rooms greater intimacy and a self-contained character, something also expressed in their colour schemes. Thus the walls of the royal apartments in the Neues Palais are typically lined with heavy, multi-coloured brocades shot with gold and silver. In his apartments in Sanssouci, on the other hand, the king opted for coloured damasks.

High-ranking guests approached the king through a specific sequence of rooms. After the Lower Vestibule and the Gallery of Mirrors the guest entered two royal antechambers. The king's private access to his rooms was through the library. No apartments were planned for his wife, Queen Elisabeth Christine. After their marriage she was granted the palace of Schönhausen near Berlin, to which she retired after her estrangement from the king. The king's apartments were tailored both to his needs and tastes. The furnishing of the rooms, most of which are small, reflects his daily routine and his love of the arts.

The Heir to the Throne Frederick William II
(1744–1797)

Frederick William II was the nephew of Frederick the Great. As the king had no children, the succession passed to his brother Augustus William and after the latter's early death to his son Frederick William. The relationship between the old king and his successor was very strained. Frederick the Great had little faith in his nephew's abilities and treated him with severity and often with wounding irony. Nevertheless, in line with absolutist tradition, the heir to the throne was given a small set of rooms on the first floor of the Neues Palais. The apartments of the Prince of Prussia, as he was officially titled, were somewhat modest in comparison with the generous suite granted to Prince Henry, a brother of the king, and totalled a mere three rooms. Guests could reach the prince's antechamber, whose walls were hung with damask wallpaper in celadon green, either from the Upper Gallery or the staircase. A large number of portraits in gilded frames emphasize the imposing character of the room. The portraits of Frederick the Great's Swedish relatives also belong to the original decoration of the room – his sister Ulrike was Queen of Sweden. Friederike Luise, Frederick William's second wife, is shown in a full-length portrait. The antechamber leads to the bedroom and the prince's dressing room. His study was converted into a bathroom in the 19th century. A cupboard was fitted in front of the original window niche and a bath and toilet were installed, in accordance with modern expectations.

After the death of Frederick the Great on 17 August 1786, Frederick William II ignored the will of his uncle, who had stipulated as early as 1752: "I have lived as a philosopher and want to be buried as a philosopher without pomp, without ostentation, without even the smallest of ceremonies…". In spite of this, elaborate funeral ceremonies were staged in Potsdam, in complete contravention of the philosopher-king's wishes.

The new king had an open attitude to modern architecture and the arts. He commissioned the neo-classical Marmor Palais ("marble palace") in Potsdam and returned to the capital, Berlin. The Neues Palais ceased to interest the court. It provided subsequent kings with accommodation on ceremonial occasions. Frederick William III occasionally stayed in the Upper Red Chambers, and his son Frederick William IV liked to combine his stay in the Neues Palais with a visit to the palace theatre. Emperor William I too stayed

Crown Prince Frederick William, the nephew and successor of Frederick the Great, portrayed here in around 1765 by the artist Frédéric Reclam (1734–1774). His accession to the throne as Frederick William II ushered in a new era of Classicism in Prussia.

The Prince of Prussia's antechamber was adorned with contemporary portraits. The walls of this bright room are covered with celadon-green damask, a colour favoured by Frederick the Great.

only for a short time, in the Lower Princes' Quarters. It was not until the time of his son Frederick William, the later Emperor Frederick III, and his wife Victoria that the Neues Palais was once again selected as a royal residence.

Emperor Frederick III (1831–1888) and Empress Victoria (1840–1901) and their "Friedrichskron"

In 1858 Frederick William married the English princess Victoria, the eldest daughter of Queen Victoria. The couple had long had a liking for each other, as the Prussian prince had met the eleven-year-old Victoria at the Great Exhibition in London in 1851. The liberal English princess found it difficult to get accustomed to life at the Prussian court. The palaces seemed antiquated to her. Moreover, the "Englishwoman" was not favourably received in all quarters. Over time she developed into a strong political opponent of Bismarck. The couple were particularly pleased when the king met their wishes by allowing them to occupy the Neues Palais. This enabled them to take their leave of Berlin each year from spring until autumn. As early as 1859 the crown prince and princess began to renovate the interiors with gilt and silverwork, painting work and furnishings for the rooms. Their budget was modest, but fortunately Victoria received an English pension of 4,000 pounds, which was used directly for court expenses. At first the little family – a son William was born in 1859 – occupied the Princess's apartments in the northern wing. When the prince's family grew with the birth of eight children in all, they moved into a further set of apartments. The crown prince and princess were very conscious of tradition and therefore treated the furnishings from the Friderician period with great care. The 18th-century furniture was complemented by modern items. Vicky, as the crown prince affectionately called her, was accustomed to English standards of hygiene, which at first she sorely missed in Prussia. She was emphatic about having the Neues Palais

Emperor Frederick III, pastel by Heinrich von Angeli (1840–1925), after 1874.

Crown Princess Victoria had her portrait painted by Heinrich von Angeli in 1874 in a costume reminiscent of the Italian Renaissance. Portrayal in historical costume was popular in this period.

The bedroom in the Lower Princes' Quarters belonged to the apartments of the crown prince and princess. By the time Frederick William became Emperor Frederick III in 1888, he was already mortally ill. In this bedroom he was nursed with selfless devotion by his consort Empress Victoria. The cross on the floor, the inscription above the alcove and the bust of Frederick III by Joseph Uphues (1850–1911) from 1893 are reminders of this period.

fitted with water pipes, baths and toilets. As the family lived in the palace until the late autumn and the old fireplaces provided too little heat, the installation of heating with warm water was begun in 1880. Frederick William and Victoria occupied rooms in the Upper and Lower Princes' Quarters. The family spent time here at social events with artists and intellectuals, but official duties and receptions for foreign delegates were also part of the life of the palace residents. In 1888 Emperor William I died and his son Frederick William acceded as Frederick III. The Neues Palais was given the name *Friedrichskron*, "Frederick's crown". But the new emperor was already mortally ill and died in his bedchamber on 15 June that same year. Just three months later, at the end of September, his widow Victoria had to vacate the Neues Palais.

William II (1859–1941) and his Family in the Neues Palais

As a child William II had always spent the summer with his parents in the Neues Palais. He had many happy memories of this time: "Here in Berlin we almost always felt like prisoners… So we were delighted when we moved to Potsdam in spring." In 1889 William II and his family moved to the home of his childhood. For the last time in its history, the palace was an imperial residence. Each year from spring until New Year's Day, the family occupied the whole northern section of the palace. The Upper Princes' Quarters served as the imperial couple's private apartments. The former Hunting Chamber became Empress Auguste Victoria's drawing room, while the adjoining Green Damask Chamber became the emperor's study and the Upper Music Room the empress's salon. Their bedroom was the former Upper Ladies' Bedchamber. The empress used Frederick the Great's study as her dressing room. A "cast-iron rowing-machine" was placed here for physical fitness, and there was an identical fitness machine in William's dressing room. The emperor's high standard of living meant that modernisation of the building was necessary. Old powder-rooms were turned into bathrooms, and toilets were installed in the spaces between walls. After 1900 the palace was supplied with electricity. From then on the chandeliers shone more brightly and the servants could be summoned with electric bells. The installation of heating by steam improved the quality of life in the palace. Furniture, paintings, carpets and objets d'art gave the rooms a lived-in character. This was the period of neo-Baroque, and the palace and its interior fitted the spirit of the age. Renovation and refurbishment of the rooms was carried out carefully. The 18th-century walls in light Rococo colours were darkened with varnish in accordance with the contemporary fashion for subdued gravitas.

The imperial couple's only daughter lived in the Princess's apartments on the upper floor of the north wing, while her brothers occupied rooms above the Upper Princes' Quarters. Their schoolrooms, the gymnasium and accommodation for tutors were situated on the same floor. The emperor and empress held major assemblies, receptions and court concerts in the Marble Hall. There were performances by choirs, sometimes numbering up to 300 singers. The annual arrival and departure of the imperial family from and to the Berlin City Palace was a lavish spectacle that was staged at the imperial railway station Kaiserbahnhof Wildpark (completed in 1906). Despite the emperor's love of automobiles – he possessed twelve Mercedes limousines as well as other cars – the railway remained the main connection to Berlin. William II had the parterre garden next to the palace converted into a driveway fit for an emperor

William II, the last German emperor, lived with his family in the palace each year from Easter to Christmas.

The photograph shows Empress Auguste Victoria in her private capacity. She is engaged in reading a letter, while holding a rose in her hand. The photograph was taken around 1900.

Emperor William II's study and conference room in the Lower Ladies' Bedchamber. The room contains a large number of paintings, the alcove in particular being over-decorated with them. Various objects are placed on the conference table, including a miniature version of Tuaillon's Amazon.

and the new grand entrance on the garden façade was adorned with 60 sculptural ensembles by Walter Schott. The Neues Palais was approached from the side by an avenue of limes with large wrought-iron garden gates, which were exhibited at the 1893 world exhibition in Chicago.

The Royal Apartments of Frederick the Great in the Neues Palais

Chandelier from the Royal Prussian Porcelain Factory, 1768.

Alexander and the Wives of Darius, 1763. The king commissioned this work from the Roman painter Pompeo Girolamo Batoni (1708–1787). Frederick the Great's preference for history painting corresponded to his literary horizons

Left: the magnificent Blue Chamber is the first antechamber in the royal apartments. The decoration is based on a design for an audience chamber by Johann Michael Hoppenhaupt the elder (1709–1750).

Following double page: Frederick the Great devoted particular attention to the design of his music rooms. They are among the most harmonious works of Friderician Rococo. An abundance of gilded carvings and stuccowork lends a festive splendour to the room. The mirror recesses are framed in gilded lattices to take up the motif of the large trellised bowers in the park. The mirrors dissolve the boundary between the interior and the garden—the variety of shapes of the garden plants is continued in the ornamentation of the furniture.

The Friderician Rococo was once again resplendent in the nine rooms making up the royal apartments. Here the visitor is reminded of the variety of forms and magnificent colours of the royal apartments in Sanssouci, which together with the rooms in the New Wing of Charlottenburg Palace number amongst the finest creations of Prussian Rococo. After proceeding through a ceremonial sequence of rooms, guests entered the first royal antechamber, the **Blue Chamber** *(Blaue Kammer)*. Its interior was based on an earlier design for an audience chamber by Johann Michael Hoppenhaupt the elder, and the walls were hung with paintings from the king's collection, lending the room a grand and official character. These paintings included such masterpieces as *The Adoration of the Magi* by Peter Paul Rubens/ Anthony van Dyck and *Alexander and the Wives of Darius* by Pompeo Girolamo Batoni. The longcase clock and the chest of drawers, lavishly adorned with tortoiseshell, bronze and a top of lapis lazuli, are masterpieces of Friderician furniture. Both are the work of Johann Melchior Kambly. The great chandelier from the Royal Porcelain Factory in Berlin completes the rich decoration of the room. Rather more discreet, by comparison, is the second antechamber, the so-called "Flesh-Coloured Chamber" *(Fleischfarbene*

Kammer). The next room, the Music Room, seems all the more festive as a result. The furnishings in the "Flesh-Coloured Chamber" include Meissen snowball vases, made to designs by Johann Joachim Kaendler, the master modeller at the Meissen factory. Their decoration testifies to the artist's boundless imagination: snowball blossoms, snowball flower-heads, pierced lattice-work, green boughs, parrots, green and spotted woodpeckers in their glorious natural colours delight the eye of the beholder in an endless variety of compositions. They bear witness to the king's passionate interest in porcelain. With the **Music Room** *(Konzertzimmer)*, guests now entered the king's private apartments. Here, unexpectedly, a garden world of gold and green unfolds. The mirrors open the room to the real garden. The rich decoration dissolves the boundaries of the room as in the Music Room in Sanssouci. Gilded musical instruments and putti making music draw attention to the purpose of the room. From the time of his youth music served the king both as an elixir of life and as a statement of courtly pomp. He played the flute and composed about 120 flute sonatas. Listeners are said to have been particularly impressed by his playing of slow movements. The dominant piece of furniture in the room is the piano by Gottfried Silbermann. The tops of the two console tables against the wall on the window side were worked

Detail from the decoration of the Music Room. Garlands of flowers and plants wind around arrangements of musical instruments on the green walls.

Detail of the fine chest of drawers in the study, one of the most important examples of Prussian furniture, for which the artist Heinrich Wilhelm Spindler the younger used tortoiseshell, mother-of-pearl and ivory.

The king's study. The wall-coverings are of opulent silver brocade patterned with blue flowers. The blue is repeated in the desktop and the naturalistic floral decoration of the ceiling. On the mantelpiece is the oldest set of vases made for the king by the Royal Porcelain Factory in Berlin.

An atlas from Frederick the Great's library in the Neues Palais—*Anville: From China to Tibet*, 1733.

The king attached great importance to attractive book-bindings. The books were bound in kid leather dyed red, and a letter was stamped on the front. Books from the library of the Neues Palais were stamped with an "S", and those from the library in Sanssouci with a "V" (Fr. vigne, a reference to the vineyard palace).

Frederick the Great had his own printing works in the Apothecary's Wing of the Berlin City Palace. He preferred a handy size of book in octavo or quarto format.

with Silesian chrysopras, a semi-precious stone of which Frederick the Great was a great admirer.

The walls of the **Study** *(Arbeitszimmer)* are covered with an opulent silver brocade, and the original decoration of this room is almost completely intact. The ceiling is adorned with silvered and painted stuccowork. The king lived to a strict time schedule in order to manage the daily burden of state business. He often wrote notes in the margin of the papers placed before him as a means of giving his decisions. Despite a life filled with duties, Frederick the Great found time to compose treatises on matters of government in addition to lengthy works of history, essays and poems. The bedroom is followed by the **Writing Closet** *(Schreibkabinett)*, originally decorated with a coat of yellow paint against which the naturalistic flower arrangements came to full effect. In the Rococo age unusual colour compositions amazed and enchanted the senses of the beholder. Sunlight brightens this room from morning until early afternoon, intensifying its radiant colours – a place which inspired the king's writing. After the bedroom in the other direction come the dining room, the small reading room and finally the library. In contrast to the library in Sanssouci, the king's most resplendent study, the library in the Neues Palais was principally devoted to storing books. The four bookcases provided space for about 2,000 books, plans and maps, many of which have been preserved. The leather-bound books were stamped on the front with an "S", those in Sanssouci with a "V" for *vigne*, or vineyard. The king had libraries in all his palaces. Below the mirrors two console tables with antique tops provided sufficient space to open works of large copper-plate engravings and folios. In the library there is a faience stove, one of the few examples of such heating devices to be found in royal apartments.

A Show of Splendour – State Rooms and Galleries

The Grotto Hall

The built-in bookcases in the king's library.
The reading room adjoined the library.

Guests enter the palace through the central portal and come first of all to the Vestibule. This is unusual, as Frederick the Great here dispensed with a grand staircase whose confined architecture would have channelled guests into a ceremonial approach to the king. The restrained colours of the room heightened the effect of the marble columns particularly well. The design of this reception room was modelled on the Vestibule in Sanssouci. The visitor is received not by a portrait of the king but by the sun god Apollo accompanied by the Muses. The painting on the ceiling is by Johann Christoph Frisch. Entry into the following room, the Grotto Hall *(Grottensaal)* came as a surprise to guests. The artists used an abundance of colour, materials and forms to create a fantastical grotto. This garden room on the ground floor of the palace opens onto the parterre garden and the park. For the first time in Prussian architecture Frederick the Great here used the grotto motif in the interior of a palace. The Friderician decoration of the hall was originally

Fantastical sea-monsters and sumptuous shell decoration adorn the ceiling of the Grotto Hall.

Following double page: the Grotto Hall was the official entrance to the royal apartments and the Lower Guest Apartments. As a sala terrena, a ground-floor room, it gives onto the parterre garden with its great windows. The effect of the hall is enhanced by the sumptuous multicoloured marble floor. Photograph taken in 1997.

simpler than that seen by today's visitor. Carl von Gontard was mainly responsible for the design. The horizontal layers, in quiet colours, were made of marble, glass and minerals. This gave particular prominence to the inlaid marble floor, which is adorned with motifs of plants and animals from the marine world and shell ornaments. This impressive work was carried out by Johann Melchior Kambly and Matthias Müller. The king used materials from Silesia both in the Vestibule and the Grotto Hall in order to demonstrate his newly-acquired riches. The hall assumed its present opulence under the later emperors William I and especially William II, and contains more than 20,000 minerals, precious stones, fossils, shells and ammonites. Behind the collection lay a desire for courtly display, a passion for collecting and scientific interest. All Prussian rulers after Frederick the Great left their mark here. On the north wall of the chamber, for example, is mica schist from William II's Nordic travels.

The Marble Gallery

The Marble Gallery *(Marmorgalerie)* adjoins the Grotto Hall and is the official entrance to the royal apartments. The banqueting halls of the Middle Ages gave way, in the Baroque era, to lavish staterooms. Inspired by French models, and above all by Versailles with its famous Hall of Mirrors, such halls of state also began to appear in German palaces. Frederick the Great took a detailed interest in the subject of galleries and influenced Gontard's architectural designs. The Marble Gallery is one of the most important interiors of Fridericician Rococo.

The room has a clear structure. Opposite the tall, narrow windows are mirrors of the same height and width, which are framed by a gilded latticework also of mirrored glass and which reflect the garden. To those who walked through the gallery this created the impression of a garden space opening up on both sides. The elegance and festive character of the gallery, which was used as a dining hall, are emphasized by the use of particularly precious materials. The walls are adorned with sheets of rosso coralino marble in white Carrara marble surrounds. This choice of material is repeated in the floor. The ceiling paintings by Bernhard Christian Rode depict allegories of the times of day. The sun god Apollo, who in Roman mythology drives the

Hercules and Antaeus, a bronze statuette after Giovanni da Bologna (16th century), stands on one of the console tables in the Marble Gallery. Hercules' battle with the son of Poseidon and Gaia, Mother Earth, is depicted in a realistic and notably dynamic manner. Hercules was able to defeat Antaeus only by tearing him away from his source of strength, his mother. It is this dramatic moment that the artist has captured in his bronze.

The Marble Gallery is one of the most important works of Fridericien Rococo. Frederick the Great took a close interest in the interior design and aesthetic effect of his official reception rooms. Starting with the Music Room in Rheinsberg Palace, he evolved his ideas in the Golden Gallery at Charlottenburg, the interiors in the Neues Palais and lastly the New Chambers in Sanssouci park.

four-horsed chariot of the sun and brings light to mankind, receives the king's guests. He is followed by Aurora, goddess of the dawn. The painter's imaginative and in part even ironic depictions of human characteristics are entirely in the Rococo manner. Little putti awake from sleep, while others oversleep and are woken roughly by the wind. The goddess herself is resplendent in the glory of the morning. The sequence of paintings culminates in the goddess of darkness who is put in her place by Luna, the moon

goddess. With blue-black, the colour of the night, the composition provides a counterpoint to the glowing white-yellow of the sunlit day.

The Marble Hall

The essential architectural scheme of the Marble Hall *(Marmorsaal)*, the grandest of the rooms of state in the Neues Palais, had already been established before the Seven Years' War. It belongs to the tradition of Prussian staterooms. Its design is especially closely related to that of the Marble Hall in the City Palace in Potsdam. The king commissioned Gontard to decorate the hall, but the king's own influence on the design should not be underestimated. The Marble Hall rises to the height of two storeys and its size alone is impressive. As in the City Palace, the walls are clad in Silesian marble from Frederick's own territory rather than with expensive foreign marble. The musicians' gallery above the great entrance door emphasizes the central axis of the hall and, firmly in the Baroque manner, a glance through the window reveals the main avenue that runs through the gardens and ends at an obelisk that can be seen from afar. The king commissioned the four large paintings as early as 1755 from three French artists in Paris and his court painter Antoine Pesne. They depict scenes from the works of the Roman poet Ovid, including *The Judgement of Paris* and *The Abduction of Helen*. The pilasters structuring the walls create an ideal transition to the vaulted ceiling, whose effect is further enhanced by its ornamentation. The ceiling vault appears to open up into the celestial realm of the Olympian gods, with its painting on canvas of *Ganymede being led up to Olympus by Hebe* by the court painter Charles Amédée van Loo.

The cornice is enlivened by cupids at play. The floor of the Marble Hall, like that of the Grotto Hall, was laid in precious materials. Kambly carried out the fine marble inlays to a design by Gontard. Luxuriant shell motifs – rocailles – link up the geometric shapes, and naturalistic motifs such as flowers and leaves are sparingly integrated into the ornamentation. The marble

Above left: the division of the ceiling painting into three sections in the Marble Gallery in the Neues Palais was inspired by the ceiling in the Small Gallery in Sanssouci. The cycle *Night, Morning and Midday* was painted by Bernhard Christian Rode (1725–1797). The detail shown here depicts Aurora, the goddess of dawn. She symbolises the beginning of the day.

Above: the Marble Hall, the principal stateroom in the Neues Palais, shines in festive splendour. Fully in line with Baroque tradition, it provides a magnificent statement of royal might.

Right: the precious inlaid marble floor with naturalistic flower motifs is the work of Johann Melchior Kambly (1718–1783).

Following double page: the ceiling painting by court artist Charles Amédée van Loo (1719–1795) of *Ganymede being led up to Olympus by Hebe* is set within a broad expanse of gilded stucco. The artist particularly emphasizes the main figure of Zeus, the father of the gods, by means of red draperies. The boy Ganymede kneels next to him. Hebe explains to him his task as Zeus' cupbearer.

statues by Bartolomeus Eggers, made between 1680 and 1688 at the bidding of the Great Elector for the Alabaster Hall of the City Palace in Berlin, are later additions. They portray four famous emperors, Julius Caesar, Constantine, Charlemagne and Rudolph II of Habsburg, as well as electors of Brandenburg.

The Upper Gallery

The Upper Gallery *(Obere Galerie)*, which is identical in size to the Marble Gallery below it, lies next to the Marble Hall. After the cold magnificence of the Marble Hall, this interior makes a much warmer impression thanks to the delicate pink of the walls and a floor of white beech and rosewood. Details such as the medallions containing antique busts reveal the classical influences on the design. The richness of this room is underlined by its six paintings by Italian masters of the 17th century. They were executed by Guido Reni, Giordano Luca and Artemisia Gentileschi and depict scenes from Roman history and mythology. Ornate chandeliers give the room an especially festive splendour. Johann Christian Hoppenhaupt the younger designed the decoration of the room. He had already worked in Sanssouci with his elder brother Johann Michael. Many rooms in the Neues Palais are masterpieces showing the extraordinary and imaginative artistry of these two brothers.

The painting *Bathsheba Bathing* by Artemisia Gentileschi (1693– c. 1652), along with five other works by Italian artists, forms part of the main decoration of the Upper Gallery. The biblical story of Bathsheba, whose beauty enchanted King David, was a particularly popular subject in Baroque art. As a woman artist herself, the Italian Artemisia Gentileschi characteristically chose themes with women as their focus.

The Upper Gallery adjoins the Marble Hall. Coming from an atmosphere of cool ostentation, guests entering the gallery were greeted with the warm colours of the walls and floor.

The Palace Theatre: "10,000 thalers, no more…!"

This is the sum which Frederick the Great was willing to invest in his *Schlosstheater*, the palace theatre in the Neues Palais. "…anything more would be excessive," was the brusque instruction to his architect Carl von Gontard in one of his notorious marginal notes. The great period of theatre under Frederick the Great in the years before the Seven Years' War was almost over by the time he came to plan the theatre in the Neues Palais in 1765/66. The first designs were placed in the hands of Carl von Gontard, who in 1764 had taken over from Heinrich Ludwig Manger and Johann Gottfried Büring as superintendant of the construction of the Neues Palais. Gontard's plans of September and October 1766 failed to please the king and were above all too expensive for him, as Frederick's note of 18 October, jotted in the margin of the plans, makes clear. He eventually withdrew the commission from Gontard, who had proposed a box theatre in the Baroque tradition with a bell-shaped ground plan and a royal box, familiar to him from the margrave's opera house in Bayreuth.

Johann Christian Hoppenhaupt the younger (1719–d. between 1778–1786), *Longitudinal Section through the Theatre Auditorium*, 1766. The archives of the Stiftung Preussische Schlösser und Gärten Berlin-Brandenburg contain four original design drawings by Johann Christian Hoppenhaupt the younger. These designs form the basis upon which the theatre was completed, with the exception of some small divergences in the proscenium arch. In a contract of 12 December 1766 the artist agreed to carry out and gild the following decoration: "16 terminal figures, 15 arches with latticework and festoons of flowers, 8 palm trees on the theatre portal, 6 trophies with musical motifs between the palm trees, one decoration on the orchestra and the scrolling on the proscenium arch". This section clearly shows the steps leading from the stalls to the circle, which were removed during rebuilding of the auditorium in 1865.

Following page: view of the auditorium. The theatre in the Neues Palais is one of Germany's few remaining 18th-century theatres. It was designed by Johann Christian Hoppenhaupt the younger in 1766. The auditorium with the rising rows of seats as in an amphitheatre bears witness to the modern approach to theatre architecture under Frederick the Great, who wished to have ideal lines of sight between the stage and the auditorium as a prerequisite for perfect enjoyment of the performance. The arched openings at the level of the circle are decorated with latticework and supported by 16 gilded terms, while the proscenium arch is decorated with gilded palm trees.

After succeeding to the throne in 1740, Frederick the Great had immediately carried out the building works necessary to stage glittering productions in Berlin and Potsdam. In the City Palace in Berlin a stateroom was remodelled as a comedy theatre to plans by Georg Wenzeslaus von Knobelsdorff. At the same time building work began under Knobelsdorff's direction for an opera house for Italian opera on Unter den Linden in Berlin. In 1748 a theatre was built in the City Palace in Potsdam to plans by Johann Christian Hoppenhaupt the younger, which, with its rising rows of seats in the manner of an amphitheatre, departed considerably from the Baroque style of box theatres. Frederick the Great broke with the Baroque tradition of using theatres for festivities and banquets and gave priority to the undisturbed enjoyment of the action on the stage.

Towards the end of 1766 the king finally commissioned Johann Christian Hoppenhaupt the younger to design the theatre in the Neues Palais and

resorted to the tried and tested plan of the theatre in the City Palace in Potsdam. The amphitheatre design of the stalls was adopted and developed further by placing only the first rows of seats in the classic semi-circle. The curve of the rows behind is less pronounced, by which means the view of the stage and the acoustics in the auditorium were significantly improved. It was possible to omit the royal box, as the king usually sat in the third row or followed events from a seat directly behind the orchestra pit.

The theatre was preserved in its original form until the middle of the 19th century. In 1865, under William I, remodelling work took place in the auditorium. The number of seats was reduced from about 500 to 300.

Johanna von Sydow (d. 1792), *The French Actor Le Kain in Turkish Costume*, 1781.

The king liked to have only French actors in his theatres. One of the most famous of the age was Le Kain (Henri-Louis Cain), whom Frederick the Great admired immensely and whose acting skills moved the king to tears according to the reports of eye-witnesses. He made guest appearances in the palace theatre in 1775 as Oedipus, Mahomet and Orosmane.

The stairs from the stalls to the circle were removed and the seats were covered with red velvet. This is the appearance that the theatre presents to visitors today.

The palace theatre in the Neues Palais was inaugurated on 18 July 1768 with Johann Adolf Hasse's oratorio *La conversione di Sant' Agostino*. In contrast to Frederick's other theatres, all genres were performed here, from grand Italian opera to opera buffa and ballet to French drama. He preferred Italian singers for opera and French performers for plays and ballet. Immediately after acceding to the throne Frederick the Great sent his newly-appointed master of music Karl Friedrich Graun to Italy to hire singers. For drama he engaged an ensemble of French actors. He expressed drastic and dismissive views of German performers: "I would rather have a horse whinny an aria to me than take on a German as my prima donna." This comment referred to the soprano Elisabeth Schmeling, known as Mara. However, after hearing a sample of her talent he ultimately allowed himself to be persuaded of her quality. Nevertheless, the engagement of Mara remained an exception.

Visits by the French actors Aufresne and Le Kain were the highlights among performances at the palace theatre in Frederick's time. Aufresne, who was passing through on his way to an engagement for Catherine the Great, played before the king on 5 and 9 July 1774. Voltaire arranged a performance by Le Kain in July 1775. As early as 1767 Frederick had acquired from the Julienne Collection in Paris a painting by Charles André van Loo depicting *Mademoiselle Clairon as Medea and Le Kain as Jason*. During his visit Le Kain played Oedipus, Mahomet and Orosmane. A contemporary reported that Frederick the Great had stood all evening right behind the orchestra pit with his lorgnette in his hand and had not taken his eyes off Le Kain. Frederick wrote to Voltaire that the portrayal of Orosmane in the third, fourth and fifth acts had moved him to tears.

In his early years the king, in his enthusiasm for the performers in his theatres, went so far as to celebrate them in poems and capture their likeness for posterity in paintings. Later his feelings changed and he reviled them as "rabble, baggage, scoundrels and whores". Through Antoine Pesne the appearance of his favourite actors from the great period of theatre before the Seven Years' War has been preserved for us. The king hung the pictures in his private apartments, thus expressing his great appreciation of the performers.

The palace theatre enjoyed a period of glory once again under Frederick William IV, who reigned from 1840 to 1861. On 28 October 1841 Sophocles' play *Antigone* was performed under the direction of Ludwig Tieck to music by Felix Mendelssohn Bartholdy. The second highlight was a performance of Shakespeare's *A Midsummer Night's Dream* on 5 October 1843, again with music by Mendelssohn.

In 1929 the technical apparatus inherited from the original theatre, including five pairs of Baroque wings, was removed in order to make the stage usable for regular opera productions as part of the Berlin Music Festival. The plan failed for the reason that the costs were too high. The auditorium was completely restored during the years 1968/69 and 1989–91. From 2000 to 2001 extensive work was carried out on the stage in order to ensure that performances could continue.

With fine performances to this day, the palace theatre remains a living witness to theatrical tradition.

Anton Graff (1736–1813), *The Singer Elisabeth Mara, née Schmeling*, 1771.

The singers hired for the royal theatres were almost exclusively Italian. The engagement of this German soprano was the sole exception. Having previously reviled all German singers, the king was only persuaded of Mara's abilities by a personal audition. Charles André van Loo (1705–1765), *Mlle. Clairon as Medea with Le Kain as Jason*.

Frederick acquired this painting in 1767 from the Julienne Collection in Paris. It is a preliminary study for a painting measuring 230 x 328 cm. The pictures bear witness both to the fame of the actors portrayed and to the king's passion for the theatre. The actors are shown in the 5th act of Longpierre's play Medée, which is based on a drama by Euripides. The story is tragic in the extreme: Jason, who has gained possession of the Golden Fleece with the help of Medea, has left her for another woman. She takes a terrible revenge by killing their two children.

Festivities

No other palace in Potsdam has such a long tradition of official receptions as the Neues Palais. The great halls, the palace theatre, the smaller chambers and the music rooms all provided a suitable festive setting. During his time as crown prince in Rheinsberg, Frederick the Great had already shown a fine sense of how to stage celebrations at court, when in a letter to Voltaire he put the rhetorical question:

"What else do we do? We dance until we are out of breath, eat till we burst, gamble away our money, tickle our ears with sighing notes which arouse us to love and awake us to a different kind of tickling. We have divided our pastimes into two classes, first the useful and second the agreeable. I count the study of philosophy, history and languages among the useful, while the agreeable are performances of music, comedy and tragedy which we stage ourselves, masquerades, and gifts with which we surprise each other."

The stairs leading up to the halls of state play an important part in Baroque celebrations. They connect the starting-point with the climax—the stateroom.

Left: the balcony, an integral part of the architecture of rooms of state, fulfils a special role. From here guests could be greeted by the sound of fanfares at their entrance.

Ilse Sophie von Platen as a Shepherdess, by Antoine Pesne (1683–1757). So-called "pastoral plays" were especially popular in the Rococo period. A longing for nature, idylls and costume led to the enactment at festivities of "pastoral romances", a favourite reading material at this period.

Like many courtly dances, the minuet came from provincial France to the royal court of Versailles, quickly became established as a favourite dance of Louis XIV and went on from there to conquer the courts of European ruling dynasties.

In the Baroque age, the 17th and 18th century, the calendar of celebrations could not be too full in some places. In addition to birthdays, name days and anniversaries, there were also politically motivated festivities on the occasion of weddings, foreign visits and treaties of state. Feast days sometimes fell so close together that there was scarcely time to prepare for them. The lapse of time between plan and execution was thus very short. Contemporaries were infatuated with improvisation, as it provided a feeling of magic in a humdrum world. Neither cost nor effort was spared to engage the best artists in the land for the preparations and execution. Names such as Georg Wenzeslaus von Knobelsdorff and later Karl Friedrich Schinkel attest to the versatility of the artists and architects who made the festivities into true works of art, albeit transitory ones.

It was considered highly important in the Baroque era that architecture should partner each stage of a formal celebration. In contrast to the practice in the Renaissance period, a brightly lit hall of state was the focal point. Arriving guests were first of all greeted ceremoniously in the courtyard of honour in front of the palace. A few paces took the guest to the magnificent staircase leading up to the main floor. The steps pointed the way upwards to the ceremonial climax. After reaching the top, the guest proceeded through the vestibule and the reception room in order to reach the goal at the end of his route, the hall of state, which he entered to the sound of trumpets and fanfares. Celebrations in the Neues Palais at Sanssouci followed this typical Baroque pattern, and the world of the Olympian gods on the great painted ceiling was the goal to which all aspired. In addition to the artists, the *maître de plaisir* and the master of ceremonies were responsible for seeing that the correct procedures and ceremonial niceties were observed. Such festivities, unlike those today, could last not just hours but days or weeks, even months. It was necessary to ensure constant variety and entertainment, in order not to bore the myriads of court guests and to provide them with a fitting stage for the numerous masquerades or celebrations of planets and gods. Oversatiation and weariness were anathema, as the early 18th-century literature on ceremonies points out. One of the best authorities of the time was Julius Bernhard Rohr: "When high-princely guests are present every imaginable courtesy and delight shall be afforded to them in accordance with their tastes, their rank and their temperament, and for their amusement diverse types of masque, comedy, opera, ballet, firework, illumination and masquerade shall be arranged. Everything which is remarkable in the residence and its environs shall be shown to them."

The same can be said of the court of Brandenburg-Prussia. When Prince Henry, the brother of Frederick the Great, rather unwillingly married in 1752, exactly the kind of variety demanded by Rohr was provided. "The

tables were set with Lucullan lavishness; French comedies, Italian operas, balls, illuminations, fireworks were laid on, in short everything which royal splendour and the heart's delight could devise to make a fine celebration perfect," reported Baron Bielfeld.

The so-called "peasant weddings" so beloved at the court in Berlin under the first Prussian king Frederick I around 1700 were similarly opulent. The charm of not just making an impression and thus adhering strictly to etiquette and ceremonial even at the merriest festivities, but of setting aside the rules and taking on different roles, often those of simple peasants or idealized beings, was particularly strong.

The highlight of every celebration – alongside the fireworks, which often lasted several hours and were staged with great theatre – was above all the dancing. It was probably never as difficult to learn to dance as in the Baroque period. Whole hosts of French dancing-masters found employment at European courts, and with them came the grace and charm of the French way of life. Little princes and princesses had to learn the strict rules of the somewhat mathematical dance steps at an early age. The square, the circle and the triangle formed the basis of a varied choreography. Social dancing in the Baroque era was less amusement than a solemn ceremony and in this scarcely differed from dancing on the stage. Many dances made the journey from the country into the city, and in doing so changed their tempo and rhythm. The steps became slower and more gracious, and were supposed to be executed with the maximum elegance and seemingly without effort. The fact that this could only be an illusion is betrayed by the elaborate fashions of the period. Every part of the body had to be kept under control: "I should hold my hands so that the fingers are not outstretched, and although the thumbs rests on the index finger, the others must all lie alongside each other and not be stretched out in the manner of those who are so rich that, in order to show the precious diamond on their hand, they open out their fingers as if they wanted to grab somebody's hair or catch crabs." (Instructions for learning a minuet, 1712.)

Many dances were held in the Neues Palais, too, and although the ageing Frederick the Great himself took more pleasure in private flute concerts and intimate dinners in illustrious company, he nevertheless planned an extensive programme of festivities for his guests. The king usually regarded himself as the ultimate authority in all matters, and not only often sat directly behind the orchestra pit in the palace theatre but also amended designs for costumes with his own hand. As he wrote to Voltaire, "The whole house is full of my nephews and nieces and I have to provide them with some amusements to compensate for the boredom which the company of an old man perhaps causes them."

In 1770 he had the colonnades of the Communs illuminated with 5,600 lamps for his sister Amalie. The visit of his niece Wilhelmine of Orange in 1773 seems to have been no less elaborate and expensive, as Frederick had to pay more than 9,100 thalers for two short and three full operas, three comedies, a firework display and illuminations, as well as for the royal kitchens, the pastry cook, the silver and lighting cabinet, clothes and coffee. After the death of Frederick the Great in 1786 the Neues Palais initially lost its importance as a residence, but it was still often used for festivities. Under Frederick William III and Frederick William IV it was not only the stage for a great Rococo ball to mark the centenary of the laying of the foundation stone for the palace, but also the scene of a grandiose chivalric spectacle, the "Feast of the White Rose". This celebration was staged in the Neues Palais on the occasion of the birthday of Frederick William III's daughter Charlotte (later to be Tsarina Alexandra Feodorovna of Russia) on 13 July 1829. It was held in three stages, beginning with a medieval-style carousel with gorgeously attired riders in foursomes who competed in honour of the princess with lances and spears. In the palace theatre living tableaux based on designs by Schinkel were performed in a "magic mirror". The finale was a grand ball in medieval costume in the Grotto Hall. During the 30 years and more of imperial rule, the Neues Palais once again came into its own as a venue for glittering galas. The Lord Marshal of the day had countless occasions to issue invitations "at the command of His Imperial and Royal Majesty". For large concerts William II had a neo-Rococo stage, gigantic but capable of being dismantled, specially built for the Marble Hall. In addition to family parties, all types of entertainment took place in the various rooms. Balls, the first film screenings and grand dinners followed on the heels of musical soirées. Only the emperor's taste may have taken some getting used to: the programmes consisted of a mixed bag of pieces ranging from Beethoven to Norwegian folk songs.

Christening in the Marble Gallery: the numerous family celebrations in the Neues Palais were a highlight of the imperial tradition of festivities, with the Marble Gallery on the ground floor of the palace acting as an important location. On 11 June 1882 it was the scene of the christening of Prince William of Prussia. With William I, Frederick III, William II and the infant, this painting by Anton von Werner (1843–1915) immortalises four generations.

Invitation to an imperial gala.

The Princes' Quarters: Apartments for the King's Guests

In the 18th century rule-books specified very precisely what was required for princely living. Such works were also to be found in the libraries of Frederick the Great. For his own apartments he paid little attention to their instructions; however, in the guest quarters of the Neues Palais they were the basis for the layout of the rooms. The **Lower Princes' Quarters** *(Unteres Fürstenquartier)* were largely reserved for high-ranking guests. They extend over the whole northern half of the main building. The official rooms such as the antechambers, salons and music room were situated on the garden side of the palace. Adjoining them on the courtyard side were two bedrooms, each with its own writing closet, and antechambers. The **First Antechamber** *(Erstes Vorzimmer)*, also called the **Tamerlane Room** after a painting by the Italian artist Andrea Celesti which hangs on its walls – is furnished in the manner of a Baroque picture gallery. The paintings, which belonged to Frederick the Great's collection, were mostly grouped into schools of European painting. Guests waited to be received in the antechambers and so had enough time to admire the

Below: the Tamerlane Room, the first antechamber in the Lower Princes' Quarters, took its name from the largest painting in the room. Frederick the Great used this antechamber to display his collection of paintings.

Above right: detail from the painting *The Captive Sultan Bajazeth Brought Before Tamerlane* by Andrea Celesti (1637–1706). Celesti belonged to the first generation of 18th-century Venetian painters. The picture refers to a historical event of the year 1402. In that year Timur (Tamerlane), Prince of Asia, moved against the Mongol prince Bajazeth and defeated him in battle. Bajazeth was taken prisoner and executed. Celesti depicted a dramatic narrative in the Baroque manner. Bajazeth, imprisoned in a cage, is brought before the prince. The victors are dancing and celebrating all around him.

The Red Damask Chamber was used as an antechamber and a room for social occasions. The small gaming-table in the foreground and the cabinet are exquisite examples of Prussian furniture of the period.

works of art. At major festivities these rooms, which directly adjoined the halls of state, served as separate social areas for smaller groups. The colour of the walls or the wall coverings varied from room to room. Light pastel shades such as pink, green, blue and yellow were typical of Friderician interior decoration. The king was particularly fond of painted walls. The French wall painter Chevalier gained the king's favour and was particularly involved in the decoration of the Neues Palais. The **Second Antechamber** *(Zweites Vorzimmer)*, also known as the **Red Damask Chamber** after its damask-lined walls, originally housed Italian paintings. The fireplaces with richly decorated mirrors above them dominated the furnishings of all the rooms. The mantelpieces were worked in marble and provided an excellent occasion to display porcelain. The chairs and console tables were always included in

the decorative scheme, often being designed by the artist who had been commissioned to decorate the room. The original seating of the Red Damask Chamber has been missing since 1945 and has been replaced by furniture from the City Palace in Potsdam. The 18th-century Parisian longcase clock by Jean-Pierre Latz is richly adorned with marquetry and gilt bronze decoration. The work of the Spindler brothers, who had come from Bayreuth to settle in Potsdam, bears witness to their remarkable ability. They were masters of the art of marquetry. The cabinets and gaming-table inlaid with rosewood, palisander and types of native wood in different colours are examples of their great artistry. The **Bedchamber** *(Schlafzimmer)* on the courtyard side with its large alcove is one of the few rooms that has largely retained its original furnishings. In the Rococo period the weighty Baroque cupboard gave way to the more delicate corner cabinet. It was the work of Heinrich Wilhelm Spindler the younger and was decorated with elaborate bronze ornamentation by Johann Melchior Kambly. Kambly was extremely versatile, mastering the French art of boulle and the Italian art of

The longcase clock was made by Jean-Pierre Latz in Paris in the mid-18th century. The latticework and flower intarsia is in palisander, rosewood and sycamore.

Even today the Ladie's Bedchamber gives visitors an excellent impression of courtly living in the 18th century. The original furnishings of the room have largely been preserved.

These statuettes of *Venus and Hercules* were produced in 1768 in the Royal Porcelain Factory in Berlin, and stand in the Lower Writing Closet.

The Lady's Bedchamber. The light cast by the chandelier is endlessly reflected and amplified by the mirrors opposite it – a form of spatial illusion popular in the Baroque period.

The corner cabinet with its exuberant floral motifs inlaid in various dyed shades of sycamore and its richly gilded bronze ornamentation is a masterpiece of Potsdam cabinet-making. It is the work of Heinrich Wilhelm Spindler the younger and Johann Melchior Kambly (1718–1783).

pietra dura. His fine furniture is on a par with that of French masters. The naturalistic flower motifs in the silk wall-coverings are taken up in the intarsia motifs of the corner cabinet. In this interplay of form and colour nothing stands alone: all is subordinate to the overall composition. The carpet was woven in Halle in 1991 on the basis of the original and using old techniques.

The original carpet was made in 1765 in the Vigne factory in Berlin. The north staircase, also known as the Empress's Stairs, led to the **Upper Princes' Quarters** *(Oberes Fürstenquartier)*. The sumptuous design of the staircase is

Luxuriant silvered decoration lends a markedly festive character to the Upper Music Room. The grand piano by Burkart Tschudi was made in London in 1766.

Detail from the floor of the Upper Music Room. The original 18th-century floor exerts a fascinating three-dimensional effect achieved through the use of different-coloured woods.

Right: in 1770 Frederick the Great brought together his collections of antique artefacts in the Temple of Antiquities, which is situated immediately next to the Neues Palais. Four cedarwood cabinets in the Temple displayed his collection of gems, cameos and gold coins. These coin cabinets today stand in the Hunting Chamber.

The Hunting Chamber—a salon in the guest apartments. The chairs were upholstered in a silver brocade with a reddish oak-leaf pattern. The walls were originally covered with the same fabric, but for conservation reasons this has had to be removed.

a reminder that it gave access not only to the inner chambers of the Lower and Upper Princes' Quarters but also to the staterooms on the garden side. Entry to the first antechamber, the **Large Chamber** *(Grosse Kammer)*, was through the Marble Hall, however. The restrained decor of the room heightened the impact of its rich collection of paintings. The pictures for the antechambers and studies in the Neues Palais were purchased at the same time as those for the Bildergalerie behind Sanssouci. Frederick II principally acquired paintings by Italian, Dutch and French artists of the 17th and 18th centuries. Large-scale paintings by Flemish and Dutch masters still constitute the main works in the Large Chamber today. The court artist Antoine Pesne is also represented with his *Girl at the Window* and *Pesne's Wife as Saskia*, in commemoration of Rembrandt's famous painting. The **Hunting Chamber** *(Jagdkammer)* was a salon within the guest apartments. Its varied decorative plan is devoted to the subject of the courtly chase. The design of the seating and the console table is closely bound to the decoration of the room. Their outlines and ornamentation match the overall scheme. Weapons and nets for hunting, trunks of oak trees, foliage and animals take up the theme of hunting in imagery rich in invention. The appearance

of the room is completed by the naturalistic motifs of the porcelain chandelier. There used to be wall-coverings of rich silver brocade worked with chenille in oak-leaf pattern to complement the hunting theme. The two coin cabinets are from the Temple of Antiquities that was built in the palace grounds. The king used them to hold his collection of antique coins, gems and cameos. The decoration of the **Upper Music Room** *(Oberes Konzert-zimmer)* is also derived from an earlier design. The wall panelling was painted in delicate yellow and grey. Here too the subject of the chase appeared. However, in contrast to the Hunting Chamber, where the decorations were gilded, the carvings and plasterwork were silvered, giving the room a cooler atmosphere. The ceiling painting by court artist Johann Christoph Frisch depicts Diana, goddess of hunting, on a bed of clouds, while in the inlaid wooden floor hounds try in vain to take hold of a hedgehog. Guests in this room could appreciate the enthusiasm of the Rococo for narrative and natural detail.

Girl at a Window, an early work by court painter Antoine Pesne (1683–1757) in the Large Chamber.

Left: the Large Chamber, antechamber in the Upper Princes' Quarters, was decorated in a restrained manner in order to present the paintings—chiefly works by masters of the Flemish and Dutch Baroque—to best effect.

Prince Henry's Apartments in the Neues Palais

In the northern wing of the Neues Palais Frederick the Great ordered apartments to be furnished for the use of his brother Henry and sister-in-law Wilhelmine. The apartments comprise six rooms for the princess on the south side and five rooms for the prince on the north side. Right up to the 20th century they were used either as an ideal double apartment or as single apartments for court guests.

In spite of the alterations and modernisation work of the second half of the 19th century and the early 20th century, visitors can today still gain an idea of the splendour of the epoch known as Rococo. This period accepted the untrammelled sovereignty of the monarch, which extended to all matters of morality, taste and fashion. Access to the living quarters traditionally takes place through the anteroom.

A large number of imposing and decorative paintings were placed here on panels to which a simple coat of paint had been applied. In the 18th century a room was regarded as a complete work of art in itself. Luxuriantly silvered or gilded ornamental elements with motifs from nature were used as a means of making connections between magnificent furniture, precious textiles, chandeliers, paintings, porcelain and mirrors. Finely polished mirrors in partic-

Princess Wilhelmine's bedchamber.

ular enjoyed great popularity. When integrated into the decorations of walls or ceilings, as in the two bedchambers in Prince Henry's apartments, they created a glittering, varied and bewildering spectacle of shapes and colours. A light colour scheme heightened the impression of brightness and seemed to rob the room of any boundaries. Frederick the Great too had a preference for pastel colours such as pale blue, pink, apple-green and straw-coloured shades. "Pekings" came into fashion – delicately coloured silks, painted in the Chinese manner, which originally covered the wall surfaces of the two closets that lie next to the anterooms. Chinoiserie made its appearance in all aspects of life, as for example in the bedchambers of Prince Henry's apartments, where it can be seen on the sumptuous silks. The exotic charms of the Oriental world accorded with the new, sentimental attitude to nature of court society. Under the influence of travel literature and artefacts from the Far East, China came to be seen as a realm of earthly bliss.

The exquisite marquetry in the small and intimate writing closets which lie behind the bedchambers deserves particular mention. These wood-panelled rooms are evidence of the high level of craftsmanship and the variety of means of artistic expression in the Rococo. Flowers, fruit and musical instruments are set into banded surfaces of different types of wood in various colours. One outstanding item of furniture is the fireplace screen in Princess Wilhelmine's bedchamber. In about 1750 it was decorated by a Potsdam craftsman with coloured and silver chenille embroidery and today represents one of the most important works of gold and silver embroidery from the time

Detail of the wall-covering "Peacock with Peony Spray".

This shaving set of costly Meissen porcelain, dating from around 1740, formed part of the original furnishings of the prince's bedchamber. The pieces are decorated with hunting motifs executed in a purple paint that was very popular in court circles at that time. During the first half of the 18th century the fine art of porcelain established itself as an important expression of Baroque culture and its exquisite decoration reflects the pursuits of a feudal society. The factory in Meissen was founded in 1710 and managed to retain its position of primacy in the industry even in the face of competition from other royal porcelain factories, such as that in Berlin.

Detail of "Mandarin" wall-covering.

of Frederick the Great. Textiles for wall-coverings, upholstery and curtains for windows and alcoves were an indispensable part of the furnishings. A single type of fabric was often used for the entire decoration of a room. Frederick the Great promoted the development of the Prussian silk industry. In place of expensive imports from France it was therefore possible to furnish his palaces using local fabrics of practically equal quality.

The princess's bedchamber, like that of the prince, is one of the most magnificent rooms in the apartments. Here, as in the two closets, the wall-coverings are especially charming. The present hangings and wall-coverings are copies of the originals and were woven in 1911 by Tassinari & Chatel in Lyon. The original textiles were produced in about 1765, probably in Berlin. A repeating pattern is composed from five figural scenes and plant ornaments, creating a far-off world of pagodas, fantastical beasts and Chinamen drinking tea or hunting. Flowers and tendrils connect all the elements together. A simpler material, calico, was chosen for the walls of the closets. Here the decorative motifs, peacocks and pheasants in sprays of peonies, are printed onto a cream-coloured background. This wall-covering, made in Berlin in 1865, replaced the "Pekings" of yellow silk which were originally fitted.

"His simple manner, the charm of his conversation and his obliging character made him loved by all. When talking to him one quickly forgot his unsightly stature, the irregularity of his eyes and his unpleasant facial features, which initially seemed repulsive. His spirit ennobled his body, and one saw in him only a great man and a lovable person. Scholars called upon his intellect, artists upon his taste, politicians and soldiers upon his experience, poets vied for his applause and showered praise upon him." (Count Ségur, French envoy, 1784). This refers to Prince Henry, born Friedrich Ludwig Heinrich in Berlin in 1726, the thirteenth child of the Prussian royal couple Frederick William I and Sophie Dorothea. He died in 1802 in Rheinsberg Palace, where he had lived for more than 50 years and which he had furnished and designed to his own taste. Rheinsberg was for Henry above all a place where he was personally at liberty. As a soldier and diplomat he served his royal brother Frederick the Great and shared the king's love of French culture as well as his passion for music, theatre, architecture and the art of the garden. Only on rare occasions did he comply with Frederick the Great's commands to attend court functions in Berlin and Potsdam and thus to visit the Neues Palais.

Prince Henry of Prussia, bronze bust from the prince's bedchamber, 1789.

A work by Jean Antoine Houdon (1741–1828) was the model for this bronze cast by Houdon's pupil Pierre Philippe Tumire, executed in 1789 during Prince Henry's second trip to Paris in pre-revolutionary France. The original had been made in Houdon's studio five years previously during Henry's first visit to the French capital. The artist accurately captures the prince's character and portrays him with great realism.

Life in the Palace

The Communs

Away from the majestic halls and impressive suites of state rooms lay the quarters where the servants worked and lived. Surviving records, documenting titles such as lord marshal, lamp master, court pastry-cook, salter of game, wine cellarer and silver butler, attest to the variety of functions at the royal court. The courtly household had for centuries been based in the City Palace in Berlin. Only as a result of territorial expansion were other households established away from Berlin. From 1769 these included the Neues Palais.

Johann Friedrich Meyer (1728–1789), *The Communs at the Neues Palais*, c. 1770. A splendid façade conceals the real purpose of the two buildings: to accommodate the kitchens and the service areas. With their exterior entirely in tune with the complete ensemble of Neues Palais and park, the Communs represent an appropriate pendant to the imposing palace.

As Frederick the Great only used this palace in the summer months, the requirement for staff was much smaller than when the emperors used the palace 100 years later. Under Frederick the Great the service area was almost entirely confined to the Communs. The high water table meant that the cellar was not fitted out for practical use.

It was not until the time of Frederick III and, above all, the time of Emperor William II in the second half of the 19th century that far-reaching modernisation and extension work was carried out on the service areas, in order to keep up with the increased demands resulting from a larger court and use of the palace into the winter. The most important part of the service buildings consisted of the Communs opposite the palace. In addition to a large number of small and very small rooms they accommodated a great kitchen, a roasting kitchen, a coffee kitchen, a silver and porcelain room, a cold room, a linen room, a bakery and a pastry kitchen as well as living accommodation for the palace staff, court pages and lackeys.

Right: an open mirrored door, in the background the connecting door to the serving room situated in the cellar. So that staff could serve meals via a "short cut", a small staircase situated behind a mirrored door in the Marble Gallery led down to the cellar. In this way the servants and the food were quickly and "invisibly" at hand.

Warming cover from the "2nd Potsdam service" for the Neues Palais, KPM Royal Porcelain Factory 1765/66.

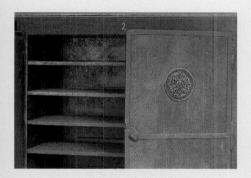

Whereas in the 18th century the food had to be carried from the kitchen across the courtyard to the palace under a porcelain cover, 100 years later it could be transported via an underground passage. Once inside the serving-room in the palace cellar, the food could be reheated in warming cupboards before it was served.

Menu for a "royal luncheon".

From the Kitchen to the Table

In order to avoid unpleasant smells and to reduce the danger of fires from open hearths, in past centuries the kitchen areas of large palaces were often separate buildings. This meant that in earlier times the dishes which had been prepared had to be taken across the courtyard to the palace by the servants. Warming covers, usually made of porcelain, prevented the dishes from going cold. For large festivities additional staff and the necessary crockery could be called in from Berlin. Under the emperors this system entirely changed. From now on the food was carried through an underground passage which led diagonally below the courtyard from the Communs to the palace. After arriving in the palace cellar the dishes were distributed by the staff via windowless staircases. During celebrations a serving room was available beneath the rooms of state with cupboards in which the food could be warmed.

Dining was not always as elaborate as the "Royal Luncheon" whose menu is illustrated here. Viktoria Luise, the only daughter of Emperor

William II, wrote in her memoirs: "The emperor ate very moderately. Our dinner was never permitted to last longer than 40 minutes. The first breakfast was his main meal of the day. There were warm dishes, lightly cooked. Fish was often served and fruit too was eaten in the mornings. Only light dishes were served at midday, too, and in the evenings as well he usually only took some cold meat."

From Fireplaces to Central Heating

When the palace was used as a summer residence in the 18th century, fireplaces and a few tiled stoves were sufficient to heat it.

When Frederick III and Crown Princess Victoria took to extending their stay into the winter 100 years later, however, matters became more difficult: "Heating became necessary over a long period, for which the existing large fireplaces were by no means suitable, as they consumed very considerable quantities of fuel yet gave off insufficient and only moderately even warmth."

Victoria, the daughter of Queen Victoria of England and consort of Frederick III, was the prime mover behind the first phase of rebuilding and

Decorative stoves were installed to heat the rooms on the third floor.

Fireplace in the Marquis d'Argens apartments with fittings from the imperial epoch.

Often concealed behind wall elements, under the floor or behind double doors, the modern heating system installed during imperial times was placed where it could not be seen.

For centuries the danger of fire was a risk that could hardly be contained. The fire alarm system in the Neues Palais can therefore be seen as extremely modern. For the first time materials and equipment to extinguish fires were placed inside the palace. Their respective locations were numbered on an imperial alarm plan, with number 23 being the Upper Red Chambers.

renovation. She paid particular attention to the modernisation of the sanitary installations and the heating. The renovation of a number of rooms was postponed in favour of domestic engineering work. In the 1860s and 1870s, for example, the first central heating was installed, powered by low-pressure steam. In essence this consisted of walled-in hearths with circular steel elements around which the exhaust gases passed as a means of heating the water. This system made it possible to heat certain areas of the palace and provide warm water available at all times. In a second rebuilding phase around 1900 Emperor William II installed the first cast-iron warm-water sectional boilers, the prototype of the free-standing boiler produced by the Strebel company, assembled from individual cast-iron sections.

Just how much fuel was consumed is revealed by a note in the files from 5 January 1895. At an outside temperature of 0° Centigrade, 30 hundredweight of coal was needed each day just to heat the living rooms of the Neues Palais.

The Bathrooms

In the first weeks after moving from her home in England to the foreign land of Prussia, Crown Princess Victoria wrote to her mother about the sanitary conditions in the City Palace in Berlin: washing was only possible in cold water, there were no bathrooms and everywhere was draughty, musty and dark. She would have found the situation little different in the Neues Palais. The facilities here were scarcely more than commodes and powder rooms left from the time of Frederick the Great. At her insistence cesspits were dug and water pipes laid for the first time, and the word "water closet" makes its first appearance in the files. Alongside toilets with water the palace was equipped with bathtubs at this period. With tiled walls, taps for hot and cold water and a shower, they were built into the now superfluous powder rooms – almost invisible and by modern standards somewhat spartan.

An unusual example of a bath is this bathtub in a cupboard. When the cupboard doors are closed visitors register only an impressive wardrobe.

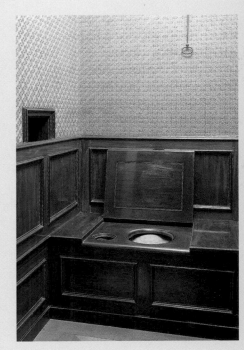

While commodes or tin buckets were part of the room furnishings in the 18th century, in the 19th century toilets were built in. They were usually situated near to or between the bedchambers, hidden behind a small door.

Next to the enormous built-in beds, small closets used as powder rooms continued to exist into the 19th century.

Palace residents of all eras liked to have their servants close at hand but as inconspicuous as possible. In Frederick the Great's time the servants' bedrooms were concealed in the wall so that they could be summoned at any time.

Always on Call: the Servants

The large number of small doors in the palace quickly prompts the question of what function they served. They do not lead to secret passages for the noble residents, but enable the servants to be at hand inconspicuously and to disappear again with equal discretion. Whereas in Frederick the Great's day the king, his guests and the servants took the same corridors and staircases, in the 19th century windowless stairwells were created between storeys. The emperor attached importance to the separation of the royal family from the staff.

The service area of the palace was situated in the northern wing beneath the imperial apartments. Around 1900 an ice-cellar, storeroom and fruit pantry were accommodated here in the coolest part of the building, with the wine cellar and bottle-washing room close by. The silver-cleaning room, the lamp chamber and the servants' own dining room were grouped around the coffee kitchen so as to be easily reached by the staff. This was not without disturbance for the emperor living above. Thus William II issued instructions through the marshal of the court that "unnecessary noise, especially the hasty slamming of doors, is to be avoided. Yesterday the noise on the lower floor was so great that his Imperial Majesty was disturbed, and was compelled to order quiet in person."

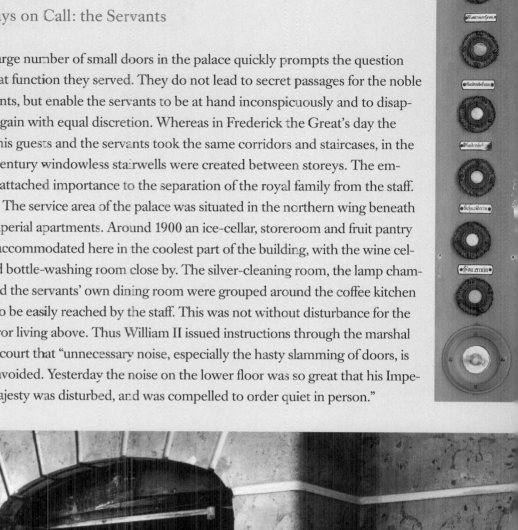

Royal pages at the court of Frederick William IV.

Above right: a large body of servants was responsible for the daily routine of the palace. The innovation of electricity made it possible to ring for them by pressing a button. The old speaking-tube was almost obsolete.

The imperial family's private apartments took up the whole of the north wing. The passenger lift with its little bench permitting comfortable transportation was right up to date.

Front cover: Neues Palais, garden façade
Front cover fold: *Frederick the Great*, marble bust, 1770
Inside front cover: plan of Sanssouci park and floor plans of the Neues Palais
(mapping and plans © SPSG Michael Benecke)
Inside back cover: family tree of the rulers of the house of Hohenzollern from
Elector Frederick William of Brandenburg to Emperor William II.

Since its foundation in 1994, the Stiftung Preußische Schlösser und Gärten Berlin-Brandenburg
has endeavoured to remodel the palace interiors with reference to the original inventory
which is still extant. In the Neues Palais this process has not been completed. Changes from
the room descriptions can therefore not be ruled out.

Photographic credits: all illustrations are from the archives of the Stiftung Preußische
Schlösser und Gärten Berlin-Brandenburg (photographers: Klaus Bergmann, Roland Handrick,
Gerhard Murza, Wolfgang Pfauder and others) with the following exceptions:
Brandenburgisches Landesamt für Denkmalpflege und Archäologisches Landesmuseum,
Messbildarchiv: page 21;
© Klaus Frahm/artur: title page, page 2 top left and centre right, 6–7, 10 left, 10–11, 22, 28, 29,
30–31, 35 bottom, 38 left, 50 bottom, back cover top left and centre right;
Hagen Immel, Potsdam: front cover, front cover fold, page 2 centre left and bottom left, 13 right,
15, 19, 26 top and right, 27, 34 left, 43, 49 bottom, 51 right, 52 bottom, 53, 54 top, 56 bottom
right, 57, 59 top left, centre left and bottom right, 60, 61, 62, 63 top left, centre left and top right,
back cover bottom right.

© Contents and design: Prestel Verlag, Munich · Berlin · London · New York, 2005

The Library of Congress Cataloguing-in-Publication data is available.

Prestel Verlag, Königinstr. 9, D-80539 München
Tel. +49 (0) 89 38 1709–0, fax +49 (0) 89 38 1709–35
info@prestel.de
www.prestel.de

Prestel books are available worldwide. Please contact your nearest bookseller or
write to one of the above addresses for information concerning your local distributor.

Edited by: Frauke Berchtig (German text)
Translated from the German by: John Sykes
Project management: Hansmann+Hausmann, Cologne
Design: Maja Kluy, Munich
Reproductions by LVD, Berlin
Printed and bound by: PrintConsult, Munich
Printed on chlorine-free bleached paper
Printed in Slovakia

ISBN 3–7913–3304–6

Detail of the floor of the Upper Music Room.